Opening Doors of Welcome and Justice to Parishioners with Disabilities

A Parish Resource Guide

National Catholic Partnership on Disability
Washington, D.C.

Contents

Preface

Today Christ asks each of us the same question he posed to James and John: "Can you drink the cup that I drink?"

(Mk 10:38)

While we may intellectually acknowledge that it is through the acceptance of human suffering that we are united with him, on an emotional level, acceptance of pain and suffering may seem very foolish. Popular culture reinforces our desire to avoid discomfort and seek worldly success and the admiration of our peers. Such an emphasis on productivity and efficiency reinforces a tendency to discount other human attributes. As Catholics, we know that the virtues of compassion, generosity, persistence, courage, gentleness, and empathy are more closely associated with our shared fragility than with a life freed from concern for the welfare of others.

Disabilities are the normal and anticipated outcome of the risks, strains, and stresses of the living process itself. The condition is not just an individual tragedy but an expectation within any community. And a positive aspect of disability is that each time one of us feels needed and essential to another, the threads of our interaction are reinforced, and the fabric that holds us together as Church and as society is powerfully strengthened.

Our brothers and sisters with various disabilities can teach us acceptance of Christ's cup, as well as illustrate those gifts that our mutual vulnerabilities can bring into our world.

- The blind lector may demonstrate to those assembled that there is much to be learned that is not limited by the narrow range of visible light.

- Her friend, who is visually impaired, confirms that limited sight can protect her from some of the ugliness of our environment.

- A priest who is deaf proves that wisdom is not based upon what the ears can hear.

- Another who is hard of hearing may remind us that not all noise is worth the listening.

- Parishioners who are physically disabled can teach us about our ability to learn different and unique ways to accomplish essential tasks.

- A teacher who has dealt with mental illness can help us to acknowledge our shared vulnerability and ability to prevail in spite of challenges.

- Those uncounted individuals whose disabilities are invisible to us—who may completely escape our notice—can, if we pause and give them our attention, tell us of the profound lessons they have learned about silent acceptance of Christ's cup of pain.

- Our brothers and sisters with various cognitive disabilities can teach us simple lessons that too often slip by the quick and abstract thinker. Members of this group are particular targets for the culture of death, such as those who seek to eliminate Down's syndrome through abortion. Yet these individuals seem particularly essential in our competitive environment. We can learn much from athletes who love to race but will pause and help a fallen friend rejoin the race.

This parish guide focuses on assisting each parish in the nation to continue the exploration of the gifts that come as the doors and hearts of our parishioners are opened to persons with disabilities.

Miracles happen as we accept Christ's cup and reach out to those who are suffering outside the gate, waiting to be invited into the loving circle of his Church.

During his December 3, 2000, homily at the Basilica of St. Paul-Outside-the-Walls in celebration of the Jubilee of the Disabled, John Paul II spoke to the thousands of people with various disabilities assembled there:

> By your presence, dear brothers and sisters, you reaffirm that disability is not only a need, but also and above all a stimulus and a plea. Of course, it is a request for help, but even before that it is a challenge to individual and collective selfishness; it is an invitation to ever new forms of brotherhood. By your situation you call into question those conceptions of life that are solely concerned with satisfaction, appearances, speed and efficiency. (no. 5)

Certainly, John Paul II has shown us the wisdom of thought and the powerful insights that can arise out of physical weakness. But the small child who lies in a tiny crib yet who strives to survive despite multiple handicaps also tells us how precious is God's gift of life. The inspiration for our acceptance of Christ's challenge can come from everyday encounters as well as from honored authorities.

In *The Poetry of John Paul II—Roman Triptych: Meditations*,[1] in the first part, "The Stream," the Holy Father writes,

The undulating wood slopes down
to the rhythm of mountain streams . . .
If you want to find the source,
you have to go up, against
*   the current.*
Break through, search, don't yield,
You know it must be here somewhere.
Where are you? . . . Source, where
*   are you?!*

It is a challenge to go against the current, to accept the pain and challenges of life without yielding. But let us rejoice that the Source is there, beckoning us to ascend beyond ourselves.

May God bless our mutual efforts to follow Christ and drink from his cup.

Mary Jane Owen
Executive Director
National Catholic Partnership
on Disability

Note

1 John Paul II, *The Poetry of John Paul II— Roman Triptych: Meditations* (Washington, DC: United States Conference of Catholic Bishops, 2003), 9.

Letter to Pastors and Parish leaders

Dear Pastor and Parish Leaders:

In November 1978, the U.S. Catholic bishops issued the *Pastoral Statement of U.S. Catholic Bishops on Persons with Disabilities*, calling on "people of good will to reexamine their attitudes toward their disabled brothers and sisters and promote their well-being, acting with the sense of justice and the compassion that the Lord so clearly desires" (no. 1).

In the twenty-five years since this prophetic statement was issued, much has transpired that is cause for celebration. Increasingly, churches are finding creative ways to welcome parishioners

with disabilities into fuller participation in the life of the parish community. As barriers are eliminated, Catholics with disabilities are sharing their gifts through various ministries. More people are coming to understand the wisdom of human vulnerability and its power to foster interdependence. Canon law no longer excludes from ordination otherwise qualified candidates with disabilities. One diocese offers to all its Catholic school teachers a variety of in-service programs and an opportunity to earn a master's degree in inclusive Catholic education.

Even as we celebrate these strides forward, we recognize the need to continue efforts to open doors to Catholics with disabilities. They and their family members who may have left the Church over past hurts and misunderstandings need to be welcomed home. Access features are still needed in many parishes. Potential vocations need to be encouraged. What Pope John Paul II called the "culture of death" needs to be countered with positive stories and images of disability.

We offer this parish resource guide, *Opening Doors of Welcome and Justice to Parishioners with Disabilities*, to guide your efforts to build an inclusive and welcoming community of faith. Be assured that we are not suggesting that you create more programs that will burden you with added work and concerns. Rather, we offer practical tips for welcoming Catholics with disabilities and drawing on their gifts. Parishes can best commemorate the twenty-fifth anniversary of the 1978 *Pastoral Statement* and work toward future progress by renewing their commitment to create access and by making use of the gifts of parishioners who live with various disabling conditions so that they can truly join in the Eucharistic and other celebrations of the parish family.

We trust that you, your staff, and your volunteers will find this guide to be a useful tool for your efforts to open doors of justice and welcome. Be assured of our prayers for you and your parish. For further ideas and guidance, we encourage you to contact the National Catholic Partnership on Disability at 202-529-2933.

Sincerely yours in Christ,

NCPD Board of Directors
Thomas J. Blee, Esq.
Fort Wayne, Indiana

Most Rev. Thomas V. Daily, DD
Bishop of Brooklyn
Brooklyn, New York

Michael J. Degnan, PhD
St. Paul, Minnesota

Most Rev. Daniel N. DiNardo, STL
(Executive Committee Member)
Bishop of Sioux City
Sioux City, Iowa

Most Rev. Michael P. Driscoll, MSW
Bishop of Boise
Boise, Idaho

Jerald D. Freewalt
Columbus, Ohio

Francis E. Cardinal George, OMI
(Episcopal Moderator)
Archbishop of Chicago
Chicago, Illinois

Jackie Johnson, RN, BS
Erie, Pennsylvania

Sr. Eleace King, IHM, EdD
Bridgeport, Connecticut

Msgr. Louis A. Marucci, DMin
Camden, New Jersey

Thomas J. Marzen, JD
Terre Haute, Indiana

Palmira Perea-Hay, LISW, ACSW
Albuquerque, New Mexico

Grace M. Rinaldi
(Secretary)
Hawthorne, California

Nancy C. Thompson, DMin
(Chairperson)
Cedar Rapids, Iowa

How to Use This Resource

For most Catholics, the community of believers is embodied in the local parish. The parish is the door to participation for persons with disabilities, and it is the responsibility of the pastor and lay leaders to make sure that this door is always open.

—United States Conference of Catholic Bishops (USCCB), Pastoral Statement of U.S. Catholic Bishops on Persons with Disabilities (Washington, DC: USCCB, 1978), no. 18

This parish guide offers sections containing the following practical resources:

- Frequently asked questions about opening doors of welcome and justice to parishioners with disabilities
- Signs of an open-door parish—a checklist for evaluating parish efforts in welcoming parishioners with disabilities
- Guidelines for extending hospitality
- Ideas for liturgists and prayer leaders
- Suggestions for homilists
- Ideas for schools, religious education, and youth programs
- Quotes and articles for use in bulletins
- An appendix containing an annotated list of resources
- An appendix suggesting questions to be included in a parish census or registration form

Are These Resources Also Available on the Web?

Yes. They can be accessed through the website of the National Catholic Partnership on Disability at *www.ncpd.org*.

May I Reprint Materials from This Guide?

Once a copy of this book has been purchased by your parish, we encourage you to copy and distribute these resources to your staff and leaders. They can be reproduced "as is," adapted to suit the needs of the parish, or used to generate your own ideas. Kindly credit the National Catholic Partnership on Disabilities.

Frequently Asked Questions About Opening Doors of Welcome and Justice to Parishioners with Disabilities

Why is this issue relevant to us? We don't have any people with disabilities in our parish.

This is a common perception. Yet for twenty years, the U.S. Census and national surveys have consistently reported that approximately 20 percent of the population—one person in five—has some disability that limits one or more essential life functions. They have further found that one family in three has a member with a disability. The National Catholic Partnership on Disability (NCPD) estimates that 14 million Catholics in the United States live with a disability.

Whether a parishioner has a disability cannot always be detected by use of a wheelchair, hearing aid, or guide animal—indeed, not all disabilities are physical or sensory. You may have parishioners with cognitive disabilities (such as dyslexia or mental retardation) or emotional or psychological disorders that can be debilitating in less visible ways (such as post-traumatic stress disorder or manic depression).

If parishioners with disabilities are not currently active in a parish, the question must be asked, Where are they, and why aren't they here? In some cases, an individual has not felt welcomed, and the individual and his or her family members have left the parish. In other cases, barriers prevent participation—such as steps, inaccessible restrooms, small-print missalettes, lack of transportation, or lack of accommodation for the deaf or hard-of-hearing. In addition, aging individuals who may not report themselves as having a disability often experience diminished mobility, vision, and hearing, which can be greatly enhanced by adequate lighting, hearing enhancement systems, railings, and ramps.

Catholics with disabilities will seek and be grateful to attend a parish that offers access and a welcoming atmosphere.

How do I identify disabled parishioners and assess their needs?

Once a parish commits to welcoming those with disabilities, it can reach out in many ways. Most important, parishioners should be encouraged to invite family members or friends who may have a disability. Other ways to reach out include the following:

- Place articles in the bulletin and possibly the diocesan newspaper.

- Indicate accessibility features (such as wheelchair access or sign-language interpreters) on fliers advertising events and on the parish website.

- Visit residential facilities near the parish to extend an invitation and offer transportation, if possible.

- Visit independent-living centers and agencies providing services.

Parish census or registration materials should include the questions noted in Appendix B of this guide, "Questions to Include in a Parish Census or Registration Form."

How can we afford the ramps, elevators, and other special equipment?

Many access features do not require large expenditures. Designating parking spaces, adjusting door pressure, replacing handles on doors and faucets, and printing large-print bulletins, for example, require minimal expenditure but greatly enhance access.

Other accommodations—such as ramps, Braille resources, or professional sign-language interpretation—do require more budgeting and probably fundraising. Planning is key. Anticipated expenditures for such items as large-print hymnals, Braille hymnals, and interpreters can be included in the parish budget. Renovations should be part of a larger parish plan and possibly a capital campaign. Local organizations from which funds can be requested include the Knights of Columbus state and local chapters, Order of the Alhambra, Council of Catholic Women, Knights of Malta, St. Vincent de Paul Society, religious communities, parent groups, civic groups, and local corporations, businesses, or foundations.

The United States Conference of Catholic Bishops (USCCB), in its *Guidelines for the Celebration of the Sacraments with Persons with Disabilities*, notes, "While

full accessibility may not always be possible for every parish, it is desirable that at least one fully accessible community be available in a given area. Parishes may, in fact, decide to collaborate in the provision of services to persons with disabilities" (no. 3). Likewise, the Diocese of Brooklyn, in its pastoral statement *Come to Me: The Church's Response to Disabled Persons*,[1] offers the following guidance: "The parishes in a ministerial cluster should strive to provide a full response to all the needs of all disabled persons. One church building may be able to have a ramp; another church may have the financial resources for an interpreted Mass, etc. Parishes with different facilities should then publish that information, permanently, in the neighboring parishes' bulletins."

Am I expected to set up a special program?

No. The sections in this guide offer ideas about building welcome and access into your existing parish celebrations and programs. The goal is for parishioners with disabilities to be active, participating members of the parish community. On occasion, however, a person may need to receive individualized catechesis, a decision made in consultation with the individual and his or her family members.

How might we celebrate the twenty-fifth anniversary of the 1978 *Pastoral Statement of U.S. Catholic Bishops on Persons with Disabilities*?

The U.S. Catholic bishops approved the *Pastoral Statement on Persons with Disabilities* in November 1978. The National Catholic Partnership on Disability recommends that the twenty-fifth anniversary year be celebrated from November 2003 through November 2004 in whatever manner is deemed appropriate by a parish or diocese. Commemorations might include a combination of the following: a Eucharistic liturgy in which parishioners with disabilities are active participants; development of a parish plan for creating access and welcome (to be assessed and updated annually); a special blessing service to acknowledge and celebrate parish access features (such as a ramp or elevator); articles or notices in the bulletin to highlight the contributions and roles of parishioners with disabilities or those who minister with them; a parish volunteer day to help a local program or ministry with people with disabilities; a second collection in keeping with the theme. This parish guide is designed to assist with these efforts.

While anniversaries of the statement are prime times to begin or renew initiatives to open doors to parishioners with disabilities, the suggested commemorations above can also be used to sustain these initiatives on an ongoing basis.

I sometimes have concerns about a person's readiness to receive the sacraments. How do I make this judgment?

In 1995, the U.S. Catholic bishops issued *Guidelines for the Celebration of the Sacraments with Persons with Disabilities* (see Appendix A, "Resources for Opening Doors of Welcome and Justice," for information about how to obtain copies). The preface describes the guidelines' purpose:

> These guidelines were developed to address many of the concerns raised by priests, pastoral ministers, other concerned Catholics, persons with disabilities, their advocates, and their families for greater consistency in pastoral practice in the celebration of

the sacraments throughout the country. . . . the guidelines draw upon the Church's ritual books, its canonical tradition, and its experience in ministering to or with persons with disabilities in order to dispel any misunderstandings that may impede sound pastoral practice in the celebration of the sacraments.

Guidelines also offers some general principles:

1. "By reason of their baptism, all Catholics are equal in dignity in the sight of God and have the same divine calling" (no. 1).
2. "Catholics with disabilities have a right to participate in the sacraments as full functioning members of the local ecclesial community. Ministers are not to refuse the sacraments to those who ask for them at appropriate times, who are properly disposed, and who are not prohibited by law from receiving them" (no. 2).

Specific guidelines are then offered for each of the seven sacraments.

The annotated resources section in this guide (Appendix A, "Resources for Opening Doors of Welcome and Justice") provides information for ordering curriculum material for religious formation, including sacramental preparation.

One of our parishioners is allergic to the Communion wafer. What can we do?

On June 19, 1995, the Vatican Congregation for the Doctrine of the Faith issued the following norms:

I. Concerning permission to use low-gluten altar breads:

A. This may be granted by Ordinaries to priests and laypersons affected by celiac disease, after presentation of a medical certificate.

B. Conditions for the validity of the matter:
1. Special hosts (*quibus glutinum ablatum est*) are invalid matter for the celebration of the Eucharist.
2. Low-gluten hosts are valid matter, provided that they contain the amount of gluten sufficient to obtain the confection of bread, that there is no addition of foreign materials, and that the procedure for making such hosts is not such as to alter the nature of the substance of the bread.[2]

A 2000 report from the USCCB Committee on the Liturgy offers the following guidance:

While each person suffering from Celiac-Sprue disease reacts differently to different amounts of gluten, most doctors advise them to adopt a totally gluten-free diet. . . . Given the need for total abstention from hosts containing gluten, the common advice given to Celiac-Sprue sufferers is to receive the Precious Blood alone. Priests are thus well advised to clearly teach the doctrine of concomitance, the Church's belief that under either species the whole Christ is received. Likewise, priests should recall the right which each Catholic in good standing has to receive Holy Communion (Canon 843). In the light of this right, the Precious Blood must be made available to sufferers of this disease who request it, even if it is not offered to the rest of the congregation. Additional concerns emerge when the Precious Blood has been "contaminated" with gluten either by the fermentum or intinction. In such instances it is appropriate to provide a separate chalice for the benefit of those unable to tolerate any amount of gluten.[3]

For additional information on this issue, contact the USCCB Secretariat for the Liturgy at 202-541-3060, or visit the National Catholic Partnership on Disability website at *www.ncpd.org*.

A parish family wants their daughter, who has a disability, to attend the parish school along with her siblings. Her parents contend that her disability is minor and won't affect her school performance. How should we proceed?

Begin by having the parents gather information to share with the school and parish office. The bishops' 1978 pastoral statement suggests, "Dioceses might make their most valuable contribution in the area of education. They should encourage and support training for all clergy, religious, seminarians, and lay ministers. . . . Catholic elementary and secondary school teachers could be provided inservice training in how best to integrate disabled students into programs of regular education" (no. 30). Many Catholic schools throughout the United States are successfully including students with disabilities. Inclusion succeeds when all parties are open and recognize the gifts that any child can bring to the school. Parents should meet with the principal and teachers to discuss their child's needs and the practical ways in which accommodations can be provided.

Resources are available to assist parents and educators. NCPD's two-volume set *Opening Doors to People with Disabilities* offers an extensive section on education. The Network of Inclusive Catholic Educators provides resources and training on this issue. The USCCB Department of Education publishes a Special Needs Resource Directory. The National Catholic Educational Association (NCEA) has offered "Making Room for Me" seminars in the past and has plans for future events; NCEA's quarterly publication *Beginnings* and its major monthly publication *Momentum* include reports on special learning needs. See Appendix A, "Resources for Opening Doors of Welcome and Justice," for further information.

Important life lessons, including acceptance of differences, patience, and empathy, are learned when students with and without disabilities share classroom experiences. The mutual benefit of such interaction is invaluable, as evidenced by a letter to the editor that appeared in the *Catholic Times* of Springfield, Illinois, sent by grateful parents Nancy and Harvey Schrenk[4]

> We want to publicly express our gratitude to the teachers, priests, staff, aftercare ladies and students of St. Aloysius Grade School in Springfield for the education and nurturing of our daughter, Rachel. She has neurological difficulties, which impact her social and educational skills. However, her progress after nine years at St. Al's surpasses most everything we expected of her. She has evolved through appropriate accommodations and some modified grading, but we never felt she was allowed to just "get by."
>
> Rachel is a spiritual girl so we are especially grateful she could receive a Catholic grade school education with all the unique benefits of a God-centered curriculum. Catholic schools in general are not fully equipped to handle the full range of behavioral, physical, and academic disabilities that our fine public schools routinely and capably serve at great expense. But Rachel's years at St. Al's prove that given a compassionate and caring environment, Catholic schools can and will bend over backwards to reasonably accommodate a child and a family willing to work hard enough to give their special needs child a Catholic education.
>
> We pray God will reward each of you for your kindness, patience, persistence and love. (*Catholic Times*, Springfield, IL, June 1, 2003)

Notes

1 Bishop Thomas V. Daily, DD, Diocese of Brooklyn, *Come to Me: The Church's Response to Disabled Persons* (Brooklyn, NY: Catholic Charities Office for Disabled Persons, 1992).

2 Congregation for the Doctrine of the Faith, *Norms for Use of Low-Gluten Bread and Mustum* (Vatican City: Congregation for the Doctrine of the Faith, 1994).

3 USCCB, Bishops' Committee on the Liturgy, "Celiac-Sprue Disease," *BCL Newsletter* (April-May 2000), *http://www.usccb.org/liturgy/innews/042000.htm* (accessed on September 23, 2003).

Signs of an Open-Door Parish: Checklist for Evaluating Parish Efforts in Welcoming Parishioners with Disabilities

1. Are you aware of parishioners with the following disabilities?

   a. Deafness or hearing loss
      ☐ Y   ☐ N

   b. Blindness or visual impairments
      ☐ Y   ☐ N

   c. Physical disabilities
      ☐ Y   ☐ N

   d. Mental illness
      ☐ Y   ☐ N

   e. Cognitive disabilities (such as mental retardation or autism)
      ☐ Y   ☐ N

   f. Learning disabilities (such as dyslexia)
      ☐ Y   ☐ N

   g. Chronic illness
      ☐ Y   ☐ N

2. By what means has your parish worked to identify those in need of access accommodations?

   a. Parish registration and parish/ diocesan census forms
      ☐ Y   ☐ N

   b. Contacting parishioners who cannot leave their homes or who live in group homes, nursing homes, or other residential facilities within the parish boundaries
      ☐ Y   ☐ N

3. Is your parish (including the church, parish buildings, parking lot, and church exterior) accessible to persons with disabilities?

   a. Is the sanctuary accessible to all?
      ☐ Y   ☐ N

   b. Are there pew cuts for people using wheelchairs, crutches, or braces?
      ☐ Y   ☐ N

c. Do Eucharistic ministers take Communion to those unable to approach the altar when such assistance is requested?
☐ Y   ☐ N

d. Are assistive listening devices available in the church and Reconciliation rooms?
☐ Y   ☐ N

e. Is there an accessible area for Reconciliation?
☐ Y   ☐ N

f. Is the amplification system adequate to provide clear sound?
☐ Y   ☐ N

g. Is adequate lighting provided?
☐ Y   ☐ N

h. Is there a portable microphone or lower ambo for lectors who are wheelchair users?
☐ Y   ☐ N

i. Is sign interpretation provided?
☐ Y   ☐ N

j. Are Braille and large-print materials available?
☐ Y   ☐ N

k. Is transportation provided to Mass and other parish activities?
☐ Y   ☐ N

l. Can doors be opened without great effort?
☐ Y   ☐ N

m. Are people available to offer assistance as needed?
☐ Y   ☐ N

n. Are all doors at least 32 inches wide?
☐ Y   ☐ N

o. Are there grab-bars in the restroom stalls?
☐ Y   ☐ N

4. Are the talents of parishioners with disabilities recognized and used? Are they invited to serve the parish as...

a. Altar servers?
☐ Y   ☐ N

b. Lectors?
☐ Y   ☐ N

c. Eucharistic ministers?
☐ Y   ☐ N

d. Ushers/hospitality ministers?
☐ Y   ☐ N

e. Gift bearers?
☐ Y   ☐ N

f. Catechists?
☐ Y   ☐ N

g. Music ministers?
☐ Y   ☐ N

h. Pastoral or finance council members?
    ☐ Y   ☐ N

i. Social justice or other committee members?
    ☐ Y   ☐ N

5. **Are people with disabilities included in your parish school and religious education programs as students and as teachers?**
    ☐ Y   ☐ N

a. Do teachers and catechists receive in-service on providing support to students with disabilities?
    ☐ Y   ☐ N

b. Is follow-up provided to the teachers and catechists of students with disabilities?
    ☐ Y   ☐ N

c. Do adult faith formation programs include parishioners with disabilities?
    ☐ Y   ☐ N

6. **What is being done in your parish to promote disability awareness and sensitivity? During the past year, has this been the subject of . . .**

a. Homilies?
    ☐ Y   ☐ N

b. Prayers of the Faithful?
    ☐ Y   ☐ N

c. Information meetings/ parish workshops?
    ☐ Y   ☐ N

d. School and faith formation programs?
    ☐ Y   ☐ N

e. In-service for teachers and catechists?
    ☐ Y   ☐ N

f. Bulletin inserts and articles?
    ☐ Y   ☐ N

7. **For the purpose of referral, are parish staff members aware of community agencies for people with disabilities?**

    ☐ Y   ☐ N

8. **What is being done to minister to families who have members with disabilities?**

a. Is there support when a disability is first identified?
    ☐ Y   ☐ N

b. Is ongoing support provided?
    ☐ Y   ☐ N

c. Is the return of a person following a serious illness celebrated/ acknowledged by the community?
    ☐ Y   ☐ N

Guidelines for Extending Hospitality

Hospitality is more than a courtesy. A central component of the Christian message, attitude, and behavior, hospitality is integral to parish liturgical celebrations and other gatherings. Ushers and/or greeters, committee chairs, and other leaders have the unique privilege and the responsibility to create this cordial and welcoming environment for the parish community.

Each of us has a need to belong and be included. People with disabilities want to be included and involved like other parishioners. They have gifts and strengths to offer to the worshiping community. Those who are the first to welcome parishioners have a rich opportunity to recognize and acknowledge the gifts of a parishioner who has a disability. Such leaders may help a parish to dispel attitudinal and physical barriers that hinder some people from participating fully.

The following suggestions can help all of us make a parish warmer and more accommodating to persons with disabilities:

- Acknowledge people with disabilities.

- Speak directly to the person. Don't treat a companion as the intermediary.

- Offer a warm smile, friendly conversation, and a handshake to create a welcoming environment.

- Offering assistance is never wrong—but **listen** to the response and **abide by it**.

- Do not take hold of a person who is using crutches, a walker, or a white cane unless he or she indicates a need for assistance. Such an action may startle a person or cause loss of balance.

- When lifting a wheelchair, follow the person's instructions completely and without question.

- Do not touch or move wheelchairs or crutches or other devices out of reach of the person who uses them. These are extensions of one's person and should be treated as such.

- Seat parishioners with disabilities with family and friends. (Having some shorter pews interspersed throughout the church allows more flexible seating for those in wheelchairs.)

- Ask the person where he or she would like to receive Communion, and make the Eucharistic minister aware of this.

- In conversation, speak in a normal tone—shouting makes words less intelligible.

- Have pen and paper available— sometimes a written message is the best communication.

- Become acquainted with the location and operation of assistive listening devices.

- When greeting someone with a visual impairment, identify yourself.

- Give directions and explanations clearly and simply. ("Go up the center aisle and down the outside aisle.")

- If a person wishes to be led, offer an arm, walk slightly ahead, and proceed normally, avoiding sudden or jerky movements.

- Offer assistance during Communion by extending an elbow; never grab or push.

- Offer the parish bulletin, whether or not you think a person can read or comprehend it.

- Offer Braille or large-print worship aids, bulletins, and hymnals if they're available.

- Identify parishioners who can assist persons with disabilities by sharing a hymnal, explaining the service, extending invitations to socials, and making appropriate introductions.

- Invite a person with a disability to **share in the ministry of hospitality!**

(These suggestions have been included in various issues of *NCPD National Update*. A pamphlet with similar helpful hints, *Do's and Don'ts: Welcoming People with Disabilities*, by Marilyn Bishop, is available in single or bulk quantities from the National Pastoral Life Center, *www.nplc.org*.)

Ideas for Liturgists and Prayer Leaders

As the U.S. bishops stated in the 1978 *Pastoral Statement of U.S. Catholic Bishops on Persons with Disabilities*, "it is essential that all forms of the liturgy be completely accessible to persons with disabilities, since these forms are the essence of the spiritual tie that binds the Christian community together. To exclude members of the parish from these celebrations of the life of the Church, even by passive omission, is to deny the reality of that community" (no. 23).

Physical access is certainly an important component of welcoming persons with disabilities into liturgical celebrations. However, the bishops reminded us, "accessibility involves far more than physical alterations to parish buildings. . . . The experiences and needs of persons with disabilities vary. For some with significant disabilities, special liturgies may be appropriate. Others will not require such liturgies, but will benefit if certain equipment and services are made available to them" (no. 23). Such equipment and services include sign language or other provision for those who are deaf or hard-of-hearing, large-print or Braille worship aids, and confessionals or confession rooms that can accommodate those with physical or sensory disabilities.

In addition, the liturgical ministries should be open, where appropriate, to all people with disabilities. The bishops' pastoral statement states that people with disabilities "have the same duty as all members of the community to do the Lord's work in the world, according to their God-given talents and capacities" (no. 17). Providing appropriate accommodations allows a parishioner with a disability to participate in the same way that others take for granted. For example, those who are blind can proclaim the readings if they read Braille and if the text is prepared in Braille beforehand. A person who is deaf or who uses a wheelchair can be a Eucharistic minister or a lector. Those who are developmentally disabled can serve the community as ministers of hospitality (or ushers), as altar servers, or as Eucharistic ministers. Priests and deacons who are blind or deaf or who use a wheelchair preside at the Eucharist. And anyone should be able to participate in the offertory procession at Mass.

PLANNING AN AWARENESS MASS[1]

An Awareness Mass is an opportunity for a parish to celebrate the gifts and talents that persons with disabilities offer. The involvement of people with all disabilities in this opportunity, including planning, is acceptable and preferred.

People arriving for Mass are met by greeters who distribute the printed program. The ushers can assist people with seating options. Disability awareness and justice concerns should be integrated into the liturgy through the call to worship, penitential rite, intercessions, and music. The theme is based on readings within the liturgical cycle. Use these readings from the liturgy, and refer also to homily ideas in this guide.

Call to Worship

Priest: Today our parish is celebrating an Awareness Mass for Persons with Disabilities. We are called to examine our place of worship and to promote greater access to all aspects of parish life for any person with any disabling condition. We will renew our commitment to work toward full participation of people with disabilities and their families in the life and worship of our church.

Penitential Rite

Priest: Lord Jesus, you call us to follow your commandments by loving and respecting one another despite our weaknesses and differences.

All: Lord, have mercy.

Priest: Lord Jesus, our faith in you is ever in our hearts and on our lips.

All: Christ, have mercy.

Priest: Lord Jesus, you have called us to face the issues that can separate us due to race, culture, class or human condition.

All: Lord, have mercy.

Intercessions

Priest: Let us now present our petitions to our God, who knows us in our weaknesses and our limitations:

℟. Lord, hear our prayer.

Minister: That Pope N., our Bishop N., and all clergy, through their lives and preaching, will bear witness to God's concern for every person he has created and redeemed through his Son, let us pray to the Lord. ℟.

That President N. and all in public service will take seriously their responsibility to protect the lives of all God's people, from conception to natural death, let us pray to the Lord. ℟.

That each of us embrace with love all of God's people regardless of race, color, disability, or religious belief, let us pray to the Lord. ℞.

That all people with disabilities, their families, and their caregivers may know God's love and care, let us pray to the Lord. ℞.

That each of us may share our faith with all members of our Church family, supporting each other by friendship and love, let us pray to the Lord. ℞.

That our society and communities learn to recognize and meet others first and foremost as persons of equal dignity, let us pray to the Lord. ℞.

That those who are sick in body, mind, or spirit may come to know the love of Jesus, who chooses those the world sees as weak and unproductive and thereby confirms the power of the powerless, let us pray to the Lord. ℞.

Priest: Loving God, you teach us that the power of the Holy Spirit means more than any human limitation or weakness. Through our surrender to your will, may we bear witness to the truth that the source of our human dignity is not the outward condition of the body but our likeness to the Creator. We ask this through Christ, our Lord. Amen.

Music
"Prayer of St. Francis" (Oregon Catholic Press [OCP])
"Gather Us In" (GIA)
"I Have Loved You" (OCP)
"God Has Chosen Me" (OCP)
"Blest Are They" (GIA)
"You Are Mine" (GIA)

PRAYER SERVICES/BIBLE STUDY
The following references may be used for prayer services and Bible study.

Matthew 8:17
"He took away our infirmities, and bore our diseases."

Isaiah 53:4
"Yet it was our infirmites that he bore, our sufferings that he endured, While we thought of him as stricken as one smitten by God and afflicted."

Galatians 4:13-14
"You know that it was because of a physical illness that I originally preached the gospel to you, and you did not show disdain or contempt

because of the trial caused you by my physical condition, but rather you received me as an angel of God, as Christ Jesus."

CELEBRATING ACCESS

Efforts to create access through such accommodations as ramps, elevators, enhanced hearing systems, and large-print hymnals should be acknowledged and celebrated. The Access Blessing below can be adapted to bless any new accommodations and can be used as a stand-alone service or adapted for inclusion within Eucharistic celebrations. In addition, access symbols should be used in bulletins, fliers, or other advertisements of parish events so that people will know what accommodations are available.

These strategies welcome our fellow Catholics with various disabilities into our celebrations by offering greater accessibility. This welcome provides an opportunity to explore the comfort that Christ's message gave to a paralyzed man long ago in Capernaum, who was lowered through the roof of the house where Jesus was preaching when access through the doors was very difficult (as related in Mk 2:1-12; see reading in the Access Blessing, below). We might wonder who was in the crowd that clustered about the Lord, and why they apparently failed to notice that the disabled man had no room to enter the house where

Jesus was preaching. They must have been anxious to hear the Good News themselves—but did they see a need to share the opportunity with those less able? Does such disinterest today prevent any of our fellow Catholics from joining in our worship?

We might ask what role the man's family played, as well. Were they advocates or merely passive participants in the actions that we examine in Mark's reading? And what of the man himself? Had he heard of this man of Galilee who was preaching of God's Kingdom on earth and ministering to those who needed his healing touch? Had this individual—living with an impairment that would have severely limited his value to the family and community—taken an active role, or did he passively accept others' decision that Jesus could help him? We are told that Jesus cited the faith of the man's friends as the reason for the healing. All must have been filled with joy at the transformation, but again, we can only guess at the discussions that followed upon their return home.

Finally, what of those scribes, sitting in judgment and raising doubts about the legitimacy of Christ's healing? Do they remind us of those who raise questions about the necessity for the pastoral inclusion, which Jesus so clearly portrayed in this brief story?

Access Blessing
WELCOME

OPENING PRAYER

Priest: Let us pray. Living and true God, you created all that is good and holy. Be close to us, your servants, who gather here today. Be our constant help and protection. Enable us to reach out lovingly to all your children, to show understanding and awareness, comfort and consolation, justice and equality, so that together we may participate fully in parish life and worship.

We ask this through Jesus Christ, your Son, our Lord, who lives and reigns with you and the Holy Spirit, One God, for ever and ever.

All: Amen.

SCRIPTURE READING
Mark 2:1-12

When Jesus returned to Capernaum after some days, it became known that he was home. Many gathered together so that there was no longer room for them, not even around the door, and he preached the word to them. They came bringing to him a paralytic carried by four men. Unable to get near Jesus because of the crowd, they opened up the roof above him. After they had broken through, they let down the mat on which the paralytic was lying. When Jesus saw their faith, he said to the paralytic, "Child, your sins are forgiven." Now some of the scribes were sitting there asking themselves, "Why does this man speak this way? He is blaspheming. Who but God alone can forgive sins?" Jesus immediately knew in his mind what they were thinking to themselves, so he said, "Why are you thinking such things in your hearts? Which is easier, to say to the paralytic, 'Your sins are forgiven,' or to say, 'Rise, pick up your mat and walk'? But that you may know that the Son of Man has authority to forgive sins on earth"— he said to the paralytic, "I say to you, rise, pick up your mat, and go home." He rose, picked up his mat at once, and went away in the sight of everyone. They were all astounded and glorified God, saying, "We have never seen anything like this."

SILENT REFLECTION

BLESSING
Those who can may extend their hand as the priest recites the blessing.

Priest: Creator God, you give us all good things. You know our needs and fulfill our desires. You protect us when we are fragile and give us courage for each new day. You give us strength when we are weak and humility when we are boastful.

Bless this new [e.g., elevator, ramp, hearing enhancement system] and those who will use it. May it open up a world of possibilities. May it bring worshipers to our assembly, students to your saving Word, and seekers to the divine love that awaits them.

May we never take for granted any of your gifts, especially the gift of each other. We ask this through Christ our Lord.

All: Amen.

Priest sprinkles the [elevator, ramp, hearing enhancement system, etc.] with holy water.

INTERCESSIONS

Priest: Confident that we are all God's children let us approach him with our petitions.

℞.   Lord, make us one.

Minister: For creativity and sensitivity in breaking down barriers in attitude and in architecture, we pray. ℞.

That our parish community may continue Jesus' mission of love for people with disabilities, offering appropriate support and services, we pray. ℞.

That people with disabilities may respond with trust to parish efforts to involve them more fully in the life of the Church, we pray. ℞.

That we may be grateful for the gifts and abilities that all people can share with our church and our community, we pray. ℞.

That neighborhoods will open their hearts and help people with disabilities to live and work among them, we pray. ℞.

That the Lord will give us the strength to understand and accept our own disabilities, especially those that hinder our growth in God's love, we pray. ℞.

Priest: God of love, our refuge and our strength, hear the prayers of your Church that we offer in faith. We ask this through Christ our Lord. Amen.

LORD'S PRAYER

Priest: Gathering our prayer and praise into one, let us offer the prayer that Christ himself taught us to pray . . .

All: Our Father . . .

SIGN OF PEACE

Priest: Let us offer one another a sign of Christ's peace.

(This blessing, which was developed by Dr. Richard Strife of the Office of Worship in the Diocese of Lansing, was originally printed in *Jubilee Days: The Jubilee Day for Persons with Disabilities* [Washington, DC: National Catholic Partnership on Disability, United States Conference of Catholic Bishops, 2000], 8.)

ACCESS SYMBOLS

As a sign of invitation and welcome when publicizing an event, include the appropriate access symbol indicating the available accommodations. These symbols were developed by the National Endowment for the Arts.

 Signifies that a given film or videotape is closed-captioned.

 Must include typeface in 18 point or larger.

 Indicates that enhanced hearing devices or technology are provided.

 Indicates that print materials are also available in Braille upon request.

 Indicates to those interested that sign language is provided.

 Indicates accessible facilities, paths, restrooms, and parking areas.

 Indicates that a production (or Mass) will be audio-described for those who are blind or visually impaired.

 Indicates that TTY service is available for phone calls from those who are deaf or hard-of-hearing.

Note

1 This format for an Awareness Mass has been adapted from "A Litany for Wholeness," in NCPD, *Opening Doors to Persons with Disabilities* (Washington, DC: NCPD, 1996).

Suggestions for Homilists

As he passed by he saw a man blind from birth. His disciples asked him, "Rabbi, who sinned, this man or his parents, that he was born blind?" Jesus answered, "Neither he nor his parents sinned; it is so that the works of God might be made visible through him."

(Jn 9:1-3)

The reflections in the first half of this section, as well as the more specific suggestions in the second half, may stimulate thoughts of the "disability" message to be found in various scriptural readings. We know that Christ reached out to the most vulnerable people of his day. We have only to consider the fragile lamb so often portrayed draped about his shoulders. Many Catholics are swept up in the popular culture's emphasis on bodily perfection and productivity. The message of the power of the powerless and the gift of our shared vulnerability is needed as we confront those tendencies.

Reflections

John Paul II has given us many examples of ways in which our brothers and sisters with disabilities—who are born blind or deaf or with cognitive limitations, who develop disabilities during their middle years, or who acquire their impairments in their later years—can highlight the need for Jesus, the light of the world. One example appeared in his address during the Jubilee of Persons with Disabilities on Sunday, December 3, 2000:

> In the kingdom of God—Christ reminds us—we experience a happiness that goes "against the tide" and is not based on success or well-being, but finds its profound reason in the mystery of the Cross. God became man out of love; he wanted to share totally in our condition, choosing to be, in a certain sense, "disabled" in order to enrich us with his poverty (cf. Phil 2:6-8; 2 Cor 8:9).

We seek to be affirmed by worldly measures. And we receive that temporary affirmation for what we do, rather than for who we are: sons and daughters of our Heavenly Father. While we were created to reflect some aspect of his plan for us, the world pushes us toward limited perception, dependent upon external appearances and functional abilities.

We read or hear that all we need to do to feel affirmed, accepted, and self-confident is to exercise, eat right, and refrain from smoking or drinking. Yet our hearts are restless—somewhere deep within, we know that the body is frail. But we don't want to recognize that we are God's people—bent, feeble, blind, with many diseases and disabilities. Those among us who cannot disguise their fragility remind us of realities that sometimes seem too bitter to accept.

The utter truth is that we are disabled—all of us are disabled. Only God is able. Only God can create, give life, and give fruitfulness to our efforts. Our prayer and praise should come from the depths of our weakness and disabilities, not from any sense of completeness. In his first Letter to the Corinthians, St. Paul admonishes us: "What do you possess that you have not received? But if you have received it, why are you boasting as if you did not receive it?" (1 Cor 4:7).

In 1978, when the U.S. Catholic bishops first published their *Pastoral Statement on People with Disabilities*, they took pains to describe the prejudice that so often follows a perception of difference—the "us versus them" mentality. Our bishops then proclaimed the commandment "love your neighbor as yourself" as the corrective action for this perception of difference and its resulting prejudice: "We must love others from the inside out, so to speak, accepting their difference from us in the same way that we accept our difference from them" (no. 3).

Unfortunately, more than a quarter-century has elapsed since that statement was first promulgated, yet we still persist in seeing our brothers and sisters with disabilities as very different—we still often have a vague sense that "guilt" is somehow involved with their physical or cognitive imperfections, as often evidenced in healing services. As a result, we fail to recognize the spiritual gifts that accompany acknowledgement of our shared vulnerability.

Our fear of and failure to recognize our own inabilities and our refusal to accept the fact that only God is able makes John's story of the man born blind particularly relevant in a society that grows more utilitarian with each passing year. This event moves us beyond our common desire to escape recognition of our shared vulnerability; it moves us to a place where we can witness the wisdom to be found in our fragility. Truth eludes us if we continue in the darkness of sin and negative judgments of the gifts that each of God's people, no matter their disabilities and impairments, bring into our world.

Let us not be like the Pharisees, who remained blind to their sins; let us take on the wisdom of those who wish to know and worship the Lord, recognizing the normal incompleteness of our human knowledge.

Jesus said to him, "You have seen him and the one speaking with you is he." He said, "I do believe, Lord," and he worshiped him. Then Jesus said, "I came into this world for judgment, so that those who do not see might see, and those who do see might become blind." (Jn 9:37-39)

Note: The reading from John 9:1-39 is used in the Sunday Lectionary during the Lenten season and may be adapted for use during each of the three Lectionary cycles. Lent is a particularly fruitful time for parishioners to reflect upon the issues identified above, especially in connection with a collective examination of conscience.

Did You Know?

1. One in five Americans has a disability.
2. A third of all disabled Americans live at or near the poverty level.
3. The majority of those receiving the minimum food-stamp benefit of $10 per month are people with disabilities whose health is in jeopardy due to lack of adequate nutrition.
4. Seventy percent of women with developmental disabilities will be sexually abused.
5. Children with disabilities are 200 percent more likely than other children to be physically or sexually abused.
6. More than half of all disabled college graduates are unemployed.

Homilies for Liturgical Feasts and Special Occasions

You may wish to use the opportunity of a liturgical season or feast to promote disability awareness. Here are a few examples:

1. On Good Friday, the Church listens to Isaiah 53. Use this reading to reflect on the experience of the elderly and disabled in our society:

   There was in him no stately
       bearing to make us look at him,
       nor appearance that would
       attract us to him.
   He was spurned and avoided
       by men,
       a man of suffering, accustomed
       to infirmity,
   One of those from whom men hide
       their faces,
       spurned, and we held him in
       no esteem.
   Yet it was our infirmities that
       he bore,
       our sufferings that he endured,
   While we thought of him as stricken,
       as one smitten by God and
       afflicted. . . . (Is 53:1-4)

2. During the Christmas and Epiphany seasons, reflect on how Jesus manifests himself in human flesh, in all its dimensions, including various disabilities.

3. On December 3, 2000, in celebrating the Jubilee of the Disabled, John Paul II said,

> The season of Advent . . . spurs us to prepare ourselves to welcome the Lord who will come. . . . A concrete way to prepare ourselves . . . is by *closeness and sharing with those who, for whatever reason, are in difficulty.* By recognizing Christ in our brethren, we are preparing to be recognized by him at his final return. This is how the *Christian community prepares for the Lord's second coming*: by focusing on those persons whom Jesus himself favored, those who are often excluded and ignored by society. . . . By your presence, dear brothers and sisters, you reaffirm that disability is not only a need, but also and above all a stimulus and a plea. Of course, it is a request for help, but even before that it is a challenge to individual and collective selfishness, it is an invitation to ever new forms of brotherhood. (nos. 4, 5)[1]

4. Thanksgiving Day is a good time to highlight the gifts of God manifested in the diversity of the parish.

5. When we look at the lives of the saints, we are reminded of the role of human vulnerability in our lives. Can acceptance of the weakness of the human body enhance awareness of the power of our souls and our desire to join our Lord?

6. On feast days of specific saints, highlight the disabilities with which they are associated. Such examples not only give comfort to those who are experiencing similar challenges but also help "normalize" our shared vulnerability and highlight the gifts that accompany the fragility of our human bodies. If the liturgical calendar impedes delivering such a homily on a given saint's feast day (e.g., St. Lucia Filippini's feast day falls on the Solemnity of the Annunciation), consider holding a votive mass or prayer service on a different day to present the stories of such saints.

- St. Alphonsus Liguori used a wheelchair due to arthritis (August 1).

- St. Servulus's severe cerebral palsy prevented him from walking (December 23).

- St. Maximilian Mary Kolbe's tuberculosis almost killed him (August 14).

- Blessed Seraphine (also known as Fina) was unable to move her body (March 12).

- St. Giles (also known as Aegidius) lost mobility after sustaining a hunting injury to his leg (September 1).

- St. Ignatius of Loyola's significantly injured legs created difficulties in travel (July 31).

- Blessed Margaret of Castello's severe scoliosis, dwarfism, and blindness remind us of the spiritual gifts that can accompany a range of physiological challenges (April 13).

- St. Angela Merici (January 27) and St. Gerald of Aurillac (October 13) were also blind, and St. Lutgardis (June 16) wrote of the gift of the loss of her sight.

- St. Germaine Cousin (also known as Germana) was born with a deformed right hand and developed painful scrofula (June 15).

- The symptoms of tinnitus and dizziness that plagued St. Teresa of Avila would probably be diagnosed as Meniere's syndrome today (October 15).

- St. Alphais witnessed the loss of her limbs through leprosy (November 3).

- St. Lucia Filippini (also known as Lucy) suffered from many physical ailments before a painful death with cancer (March 25).

- Several saints were burdened with mental or emotional difficulties. St. Benedict Joseph Labre, who died while still searching for a religious community that would accept him, experienced mystical fits that some might today diagnose as mental or emotional disorders (April 16).

- A number of saints are known for their patronage of those who are deaf or hard of hearing, the most famous being St. Francis de Sales (January 24).

Note

1 *http://www.vatican.va/holy_father/john_paul _ii/homilies/2000/documents/hf_jp-ii_hom _20001203_jubildisabled_en.html* (accessed August 8, 2003).

Ideas for Schools, Religious Education, and Youth Programs

USING THIS RESOURCE

In their 1998 statement *Welcome and Justice for Persons with Disabilities*, the U.S. Catholic bishops affirmed that "each person is created in God's image, yet there are variations in individual abilities" (no. 2). We are called to respect the dignity of human life and to positively recognize differences. We are called to defend the rights of persons with disabilities to achieve the fullest measure of personal development of which they are capable. The bishops highlighted our common responsibility to build a welcoming Church.

This message is important, especially for young Catholics as they grow in a culture heralding consumerism, efficiency, proficiency, speed, and physical perfection. Catholic youth face challenges every day in making choices arising from similarities and differences between themselves and their peers. Teaching children and young people the core values of our faith and how we relate to one another is a critical task of parents, religious educators, teachers, and clergy. Understanding the positive contributions and needs of persons with disabilities allows us to unify and strengthen our community of faith.

This section is designed for two purposes:

1. It contains many ideas for building young people's awareness about persons with disabilities and sharing what our faith says about welcome and justice.

2. It also provides information about welcoming students with disabilities into Catholic schools, religious education, and youth programs.

GENERAL SUGGESTIONS FOR EDUCATORS

Many people with disabilities claim that the major barrier they face is the attitude of others. Often, people fear the idea of any disability and discount the abilities of those who live with disabling conditions. Thus, an important beginning point is to build awareness in order to help people develop a realistic and positive attitude toward disabilities. A first step is to infuse the message of *Welcome and Justice for Persons with Disabilities* into what you are already doing:

WE ARE CALLED TO PRAY. Have students create prayers of thanksgiving for our similarities and differences. For liturgies, include general intercessions for those whose lives may be at risk from abortion, medical rationing, and euthanasia due to a disability. In daily prayers, ask for a change of heart for those who create barriers to inclusion.

WHAT DOES THE CHURCH SAY? Have students explore the Church's teaching on life issues, rights and responsibilities, and the common good related to welcome and justice for persons with disabilities. Integrate Catholic social teaching themes in faith formation, social studies, language, art, music, science, and technology classes.

REACH OUT TO THOSE IN NEED. Encourage students to pursue volunteer opportunities at community programs supporting persons with disabilities.

BE FAITHFUL CITIZENS. Have children and young people develop the tools to exercise their political responsibility by following issues and asking elected officials to support public policies for persons with disabilities.

PRACTICE SOLIDARITY. Jesus spent quality time with people with disabilities. We are called to do the same. Create opportunities for youth to spend meaningful time interacting with people of all abilities.

EDUCATE YOURSELF. Visit your local special-education resource center for curriculum material. Such centers have instructional materials for assisting children with special needs as well as ideas for awareness-building activities. Sample ideas are presented below.

SUGGESTED ACTIVITIES FOR BUILDING AWARENESS

The following activities are intended for use in a classroom or group setting to build awareness about the lives of persons with disabilities and Catholic social teaching. These ideas can be adapted to fit the needs of the participants or may inspire creativity for other projects.

For Younger Children

A central point to emphasize with young children is to facilitate their recognition of similarities and differences and teach them that God made us, loves us, and gifts all of us in different ways.

- Stage a puppet presentation exploring the similarities and differences that are seen and unseen among our brothers and sisters.

- Invite an artist or musician with a disability to perform at school during a disability awareness week.

- Have a sign-language interpreter teach basic signs to students in a language arts class.

- Sponsor a poster, art, or essay contest around the topic "We are all created in God's image."

- Invite a guest speaker from an agency to demonstrate how service animals such as guide dogs or hearing dogs assist persons with disabilities. Invite persons with disabilities who live in the parish to share how modifications such as a motorized wheelchair or assistive listening device benefit them in everyday life.

- Fill a bag with everyday objects. Have participants close their eyes, reach into the bag, and identify each object. Put an assortment of money in the bag and have the students determine the amount. Then introduce a document such as a Bible printed in Braille. Facilitate a discussion on how persons with a visual impairment manage everyday tasks.

- Select the text of a popular story, but manipulate it by switching or adding letters and inserting extra spaces. Direct the students, one at a time, to stand up and read the selection in front of the class. Let their emotions and frustrations surface. Lead a dis-cussion on how those with a learning disability struggle while reading. Share a list of famous people who struggled with a learning disability as a student.

For Adolescents

- Have the class read about the life of Blessed Margaret of Castello. Ask students to write a reflection paper on her unique gifts and talents and how God's love shone through her actions and positive contributions. Explore with students whether Blessed Margaret would have been allowed to be born in our day, given the justification of abortion, infanticide, and euthanasia—a widespread justification in today's "culture of death," and one based on an unfounded fear of disability. Information on Blessed Margaret is available from the Dominican Friars, St. Louis Bertrand Church, 1104 S. 6th St., Louisville, KY 40203-3395. (The U.S. promoter of Blessed Margaret's canonization is Barbara Logsdon, St. Louis Bertrand Church, Louisville, KY; she can be reached at 502-583-4448.) The following are other resources on her life and experiences:

Bonniwell, William R., OP. The Life of Blessed Margaret of Castello. 3rd ed. Rockford, IL: Tan Books and Publications, Inc., 1993.

Dominican Nuns of the Perpetual Rosary. *Blessed Margaret of Castello, OP: A Mediaeval Biography*. Fatima, Portugal: Monastery Pius XII, 1994.

- Assign students to read the sections on rights, duties, and responsibilities in Pope John XXIII's encyclical *Peace on Earth (Pacem in Terris)*. Facilitate a discussion on how those issues relate to persons with disabilities. Also read the U.S. Catholic bishops' statement *Welcome and Justice for Persons with Disabilities* (see Appendix A, "Resources for Opening Doors of Welcome and Justice," for ordering information). Is our current society adequately answering the Church's call?

- Using a wheelchair, have youth tour parish and school buildings and grounds. Have them visit classrooms and other gathering spaces, use the drinking fountain and restroom, and navigate in and out of buildings, on sidewalks, and around the playground. Afterward, have them write experiences in a journal and list obstacles found along the way. Finally, have them research and suggest ways in which those obstacles can be removed, and report their findings to school officials or parish staff.

- According to national statistics from the U.S. Census Bureau, about 20 percent of all Americans have a disability. Have students analyze television commercials and shows; page through advertisements in magazines, the Sunday newspaper, and clothing catalogs; or even go to a toy store to look at dolls or action figures. Have students count the number of people with a disability in these media. What do their findings suggest? What steps can be taken to educate advertisers and the media about representing people with disabilities?

- Have students watch a clip of a movie dialogue with the sound turned off. Have students describe the scene including details of the conversation. (Even give a pop quiz and observe their reactions—are they frustrated?) Then have the students watch the same scene with the sound turned off but the closed-captioning function turned on. Again, have the students describe the scene including details of the conversation. Finally, have the students watch the scene with the sound and closed-captioning function turned on. Have them describe the scene again. A related activity is to try this lesson with a telephone conversation, using TTY technology or a relay service.

- As a group, participate in a signed Mass. Then have students explore whether their parish offers assistive listening devices and sound amplification or provides a sign-language interpreter for the deaf and hearing impaired. Discuss how such modifications can bring people into fuller inclusion.

- Plan an activity to assist your parish advocate for persons with disabilities with programs to create fuller inclusion in parish activities.

- Thirty-four percent of all disabled Americans live at or near the poverty level, and 21 percent lack quality medical care (according to the 2000 NOD/Harris Survey of Americans with Disabilities [May-June 2000]). Examine proposed legislation designed to support persons with disabilities at local, state, and national levels. Have students write letters or visit public officials encouraging them to make sound public policy that respects the dignity of human life and supports programs that assist persons with disabilities. For background material, contact your diocesan social action office, disability ministry office, or pro-life office; your state Catholic conference; the United States Conference of Catholic Bishops; or the National Catholic Partnership on Disability.

- Watch and support sporting events such as wheelchair athletes and Special Olympics. Sponsor a similar event at school or parish.

- Encourage youth to visit a residential community where persons with disabilities live. Have the students and residents share their stories and their faith experiences.

GUIDELINES FOR INCLUDING STUDENTS WITH DISABILITIES

In their 1978 *Pastoral Statement of U.S. Catholic Bishops on Persons with Disabilities* and again in their 1998 statement *Welcome and Justice for Persons with Disabilities*, the U.S. Catholic bishops underscored the importance of including students with disabilities in educational programs:

> Dioceses might make their most valuable contribution in the area of education . . . . Religious education personnel could profit from guidance in adapting their curricula to the needs of disabled learners, and Catholic elementary and secondary school teachers could be provided in-service training in how best to integrate disabled students into programs of regular education. (*Pastoral Statement of U.S. Catholic Bishops on Persons with Disabilities*, no. 30)

Parish liturgical celebrations and catechetical programs should be accessible to persons with disabilities and open to their full, active, and conscious participation according to their capacity. (*Welcome and Justice for Persons with Disabilities*, no. 5)

The passage of the Americans with Disabilities Act of 1990, the 1973 Rehabilitation Act, the 1975 Individuals with Disabilities Education Act (and subsequent reauthorizations), and other disability legislation has led to increased involvement in communities of people with disabilities. They carry the expectation of such inclusion into their parish life. Increasingly, parents seek opportunities for their children with disabilities to be included in parish religious education classes and enrolled in the parish elementary school. Youth with disabilities wish to participate in parish youth activities.

Catholic education has a long history of taking into the learning environment the rich diversity within any neighborhood. The contemporary idea that students with disabilities cannot fit into our excellent Catholic schools seems strangely alien to this sense of unity in Christ. Similarly, an insistence that each student within our religion program have the same proficiency in using resources seems disconnected from the evidence of the piety of our great-grandparents, many of whom could neither read nor write but offered up their simple faith to God and the Church.

A commitment to the vision of inclusive education is needed to successfully educate all students. Vision and commitment are the keys. Over the past few years, the following insights and strategies for creating inclusive environments have evolved and have been promoted by various national disability advocacy organizations.

Constant Components of Inclusion
- Unconditional acceptance of all children as children
- Strong leadership by school principals and other administrators
- A focus on the student's and parents' dreams and goals
- Unconditional commitment to provide as much support as the child needs in order to be successful in regular educational environments
- Educators' viewing themselves in new collaborative roles

- A focus on what the child can do and not on what he or she cannot do
- A team approach that includes parents as equal members and emphasizes creativity and problem solving
- An understanding of and belief in the fact that students don't need to have the same educational goals in order to learn together in regular classes

What Inclusion Is

- Having all children learning together in the same schools and the same classrooms with the services and supports necessary to achieve success
- Meeting the unique needs of all children in the same setting that they would attend if they had no diverse learning ability
- Having all children participating in all facets of school life
- Providing opportunities (and support, when needed) for children with and without diverse learning abilities to interact and develop friendships with each other, which helps them to understand and accept individual differences
- Allowing students who are not able to fully participate in an activity to partially participate, rather than be excluded entirely
- Practicing a method of schooling that emphasizes collaboration by melding special and regular education resources (staff, materials, energy, etc.)

- Supporting regular education teachers who have children with diverse learning abilities in their classrooms
- Having children learn side by side, even though they may have different educational goals
- Regular education teachers' using innovative strategies for varied learning styles
- Integrating related services (such as speech, physical therapy, and occupational therapy) into the regular classroom

What Inclusion Is Not

- Dumping all children with diverse learning abilities into regular classes without the supports and services they need to be successful
- Trading off the quality of a child's education or the intensive support services the child may need for inclusion
- Eliminating or reducing special-education services
- Ignoring each child's unique needs
- Expecting all children to learn the same thing, at the same time, in the same way
- Expecting regular education teachers to teach children who have diverse learning abilities without appropriate support and training
- Sacrificing the education of non-disabled students so that children with diverse learning abilities can be included

Benefits of Inclusion to the Total Community

- All children benefit from inclusion by learning about differences and similarities.

- All students benefit from strategies to individualize instruction.

- Students learn from one another.

- Learning problems of all students are identified earlier.

- Inclusive classrooms set higher expectations for all students and, therefore, get better results.

- Inclusive education greatly enhances the communication and social skills of students with disabilities, a benefit that broadens their circles of friends while they are in school and translates into better adjustment to employment and community life in adulthood.

Strategies for Creating Inclusive Environments

- Begin by educating students about disabilities.

- Involve students in creating access under the direction of the disabled student or his or her family. Encourage creative solutions to situations as they arise.

- Using a student's individualized education plan (IEP) in conjunction with a multi-action plan (MAP), create specific goals for the students. Be aware that they won't necessarily match those of the other students.

- Expose all students to the same opportunities and interactions, recognizing that the students' reactions and involvement will vary.

- Institute "no put-downs or teasing" as part of the class discipline code. Encourage cooperation and a caring atmosphere.

- Recognize the wide variations in individual learning styles, and use multi-sensory experiential methods. Use creativity in developing lesson plans, and vary presentation styles to maintain interest. Incorporate the following into lessons:

  ❑ Music

  ❑ Movement

  ❑ Role playing

  ❑ Drama

  ❑ Picture journaling

  ❑ Reflective listening

  ❑ Visual images and concrete symbols

  ❑ Group projects

- Significantly reduce—and eliminate, where possible—the use of language arts (listening, reading, and writing) forms as the primary mode of sharing information with students.

- Find ways for each student to be involved.

- Provide mandatory, regularly scheduled in-service opportunities for teachers and catechists.

SUGGESTED RESOURCES AND WEBSITES

See Appendix A, "Resources for Opening Doors of Welcome and Justice," for descriptions of curriculum materials and a list of national Catholic organizations offering resources and training for catechists, teachers, administrators, and family members.

Bulletin Quotes and Articles

A positive way to educate the parish about persons with disabilities, to welcome and include persons with disabilities, and to commemorate the twenty-fifth anniversary of the 1978 *Pastoral Statement of U.S. Catholic Bishops on Persons with Disabilities* or other historic events is to publish in the parish bulletin quotes from the various bishops' statements on disability, quotes from papal documents, and passages from other related articles. Running a series of such articles in your bulletin can help increase understanding and acceptance.

QUOTES

Vatican Statements

In Christ's name, the Church is committed to making herself more and more a "welcoming home" for you. We know that the disabled person—a unique and unrepeatable person in his [or her] equal and inviolable dignity—needs not only care, but first of all love which becomes recognition, respect and integration: from birth to adolescence, to adulthood and to the delicate moment, faced with trepidation by so many parents, of separation from their children, the moment of "after us." Dear friends, we would like to feel that we share in your efforts and in the inevitable moments of discouragement, in order to brighten them with the light of faith and the hope of solidarity and love.

—Pope John Paul II, Homily at the Jubilee of the Disabled (December 3, 2000), no. 4

It is the task of Bishops and priests to help parents, so that they understand and accept that life is always a gift of God, even when it is marked by suffering and illness. Every person is the object of basic rights which are inalienable, inviolable and indivisible. Every person: therefore also the disabled handicapped, who precisely because of their disabilities may encounter greater difficulty in the actual exercise of these rights. Thus they should not be left alone, but to be welcomed by society and, according to their abilities, integrated into it as full members.

—Pope John Paul II, Address to the Congress on Integration of Disabled Children (2000)

The Church, as my venerable Predecessor Paul VI liked to say, is "a love that seeks out." How I would like you all to feel welcomed and embraced in her love! First of all you, dear families: those who have children with disabilities and those who share their experience. I say again to you today that I am close to you. Thank you for the witness you bear by the fidelity, strength and patience of your love.

—Pope John Paul II, Address for the Jubilee of the Disabled (December 3, 2000), no. 3

Bishops' Statements

We call upon people of good will to reexamine their attitudes toward their disabled brothers and sisters and promote their well-being, acting with the sense of justice and the compassion that the Lord so clearly desires. Further, realizing the unique gifts disabled individuals have to offer the Church, we wish to address the need for their fuller integration into the Christian community and their fuller participation in its life.

—United States Conference of Catholic Bishops, *Pastoral Statement of U.S. Catholic Bishops on Persons with Disabilities* (1978), no. 1

When we think of persons with disabilities in relation to ministry, we tend automatically to think of doing something for them. We do not reflect that they can do something for us and with us. . . . they have the same duty as all members of the community to do the Lord's work in the world, according to their God-given talents and capacities.

—United States Conference of Catholic Bishops, *Pastoral Statement of U.S. Catholic Bishops on Persons with Disabilities* (1978), no. 17

Persons with disabilities are not looking for pity. They seek to serve the community and to enjoy their full baptismal rights as members of the Church. Our interaction with them can and should be an affirmation of our faith. There can be no separate Church for persons with disabilities. We are one flock that follows a single shepherd.

—United States Conference of Catholic Bishops, *Pastoral Statement of U.S. Catholic Bishops on Persons with Disabilities* (1978), no. 33

At the very least, we must undertake forms of evangelization that speak to the particular needs of persons with disabilities, make those liturgical adaptations that promote their active participation, and provide help and services that reflect our loving concern for those with serious problems.

—United States Conference of Catholic Bishops, *Pastoral Statement of U.S. Catholic Bishops on Persons with Disabilities* (1978), no. 14

Since the parish is the door to participation in the Christian experience, it is the responsibility of pastors and laity to assure that those doors are always open. Costs must never be the controlling consideration limiting the welcome offered to those among us with disabilities, since provision of access to religious functions is a pastoral duty. By reason of their baptism, all Catholics are equal in dignity in the sight of God and have the same divine calling.

—United States Conference of Catholic Bishops, *Guidelines for the Celebration of the Sacraments with Persons with Disabilities* (1995), no. 1

Catholics with disabilities have a right to participate in the sacraments as full functioning members of the local ecclesial community. Ministers are not to refuse the sacraments to those who ask for them at appropriate times, who are properly disposed, and who are not prohibited by law from receiving them.

—United States Conference of Catholic Bishops, *Guidelines for the Celebration of the Sacraments with Persons with Disabilities* (1995), no. 2

Parish sacramental celebrations should be accessible to persons with disabilities and open to their full, active, and conscious participation, according to their capacity.

—United States Conference of Catholic Bishops, *Guidelines for the Celebration of the Sacraments with Persons with Disabilities* (1995), no. 3

No one would deny that every man, woman, and child has the right to develop his or her potential to the fullest. With God's help and our own determination, the day will come when that right is realized in the lives of all persons with disabilities.

—United States Conference of Catholic Bishops, *Pastoral Statement of U.S. Catholic Bishops on Persons with Disabilities* (1978), no. 35

By Theme
LIFE ISSUES

All too often, abortion and postnatal neglect are promoted by arguing that the disabled infant will survive only to suffer a life of pain and deprivation. We find this reasoning appalling. Society's frequent indifference to the plight of citizens with disabilities is a problem that cries aloud for solutions based on justice and conscience, not violence. All people have a clear duty to do what lies in their power to improve living conditions for persons with disabilities, rather than ignoring them or attempting to eliminate them as a burden not worth dealing with.

—United States Conference of Catholic Bishops, *Pastoral Statement of U.S. Catholic Bishops on Persons with Disabilities* (1978), no. 9

A love which accepts life as a gift also accepts the given limits on our lives.

—United States Conference of Catholic Bishops, *Faithful for Life: A Moral Reflection* (1995), 15

We are facing an enormous and dramatic clash between good and evil, death and life, the "culture of death" and the "culture of life." We find ourselves not only "faced with" but necessarily "in the midst of" this conflict: we are all involved and we all share in it, with the inescapable responsibility of choosing to be unconditionally pro-life.

—Pope John Paul II, *The Gospel of Life (Evangelium Vitae)* (1995), no. 28

Euthanasia must be called a false mercy, and indeed a disturbing "perversion" of mercy. True "compassion" leads to sharing another's pain; it does not kill the person whose suffering we cannot bear.

—Pope John Paul II, *The Gospel of Life (Evangelium Vitae)* (1995), no. 66

We recognize disability and vulnerability as a normal, anticipated reality of the living process. In sharing this truth, we can allay society's fears and alleviate misjudgments about the quality of a life lived with disabilities. While advocates for death play on society's growing abhorrence of dependency and disabilities, we can demonstrate the power of vulnerability as a catalyst for building community.

—Resolution of NCPD Board of Directors (1998)

Faith tells us [that those with severe disabilities] are valuable not because of what they can do but because they are loved by an infinite God. But as we look at our society today, the condition of the truly dysfunctional, of the most severely handicapped, is becoming more and more like that of the Jews in pre-Nazi Germany. The ideology to dispose of them is already in the air. They risk becoming the object of that frightening compassion which, in this country, first finds psychologically understandable and then sees as morally defensible and then declares legally permissible and finally makes culturally imperative even the most heinous crime. The stage is set once again to betray human solidarity in the name of a sometimes sincere but always false pity.

—Francis Cardinal George, "NCPD's Tenth Anniversary Report to the U. S. Catholic Bishops" (November 19, 1992), in *Opening Doors to People with Disabilities* (Washington, DC: National Catholic Partnership on Disability, 1995)

We are acutely aware of the dangers faced by people with disabilities or advanced age in the current climate of death. Many who seek the final solution of suicide do so because of depression and fear of dependency and abandonment. Rather than succumbing to these evil practices, we must educate the public that life with disabilities and fragility is a gift to be shared within an accepting and loving environment.

—Resolution of NCPD
Board of Directors (2000)

Much progress has been made in prevention, treating, or even curing a variety of disabling conditions. However, we would never completely eliminate the vulnerability of the human organism, nor would it be such a great blessing if we could. It is by God's wisdom that the gift of life comes in fragile earthen vessels. Many of the virtues we feel are the best that humanity has to offer, such as love, faith, hope, mercy, and courage, are associated directly or indirectly with our vulnerability.

—Mary Jane Owen, NCPD
Executive Director
Congressional testimony
(April 26, 2000)

It is our common recognition of interdependency which weaves the threads of our societies together. Each time one of us feels needed and essential to another, the threads of that interaction are reinforced and the fabric which holds us together as Church and as society is powerfully strengthened.

—Mary Jane Owen, NCPD
Executive Director
*The Wisdom of
Human Vulnerability—Disability:
The Tie Which Binds*,
address delivered to the Seventh
International Conference of the
Pontifical Council for Pastoral Care
(November 20, 1992)

DEFINITION OF DISABILITY

Disabilities are the normal and antici-pated outcome of the risks, strains, and stresses of the living process itself. When we think of them this way, they cease to be individual tragedies and become an event to be expected within every family and community. Such limi-tations may occur early in life or in old age. They can result from alterations in an individual's gene code, in utero, dur-ing the birth process, or later in life. Each person's journey toward disability is highly personal and unique, just as each of us is unique. Our vulnerability, which has been encoded into our gene pool, is the catalyst which brings us into community and church with renewed recognition that we need each other and our Lord.

It is our common recognition of that interdependency which weaves the threads of our societies together. There is wisdom in vulnerability, and it will bind us together powerfully, if we will only look at the reality with fresh vision. We must constantly remind ourselves that God's gift of life is placed in fragile earthen vessels to a powerful purpose. We have only to recognize and celebrate that reality, and it will free us from past fears.

DEMOGRAPHICS OF DISABILITY

For twenty years, the U.S. Census and national surveys have consistently reported that approximately 20 percent of the population—one person in five—has a disability that limits one or more essential life functions. These resources further report that one family in three has a member with a disability. Figures cited at the July 2000 commemoration of the tenth anniversary of the Americans with Disabilities Act noted that fifty-four million Americans have some form of disability.

Advocates (such as the International Center for Disability Information) cite an additional two million people who live in institutions and are not counted in the census figures. The National Catholic Partnership on Disability estimates that fourteen million Catholics in the United States live with a disability. The chart below uses percentages from the 2000 NOD/Harris Survey of Americans with Disabilities (May-June 2000) to illustrate the occurrence of disabilities by category.

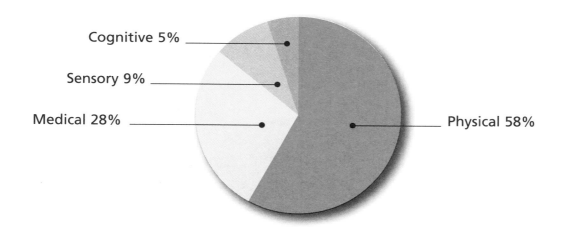

Cognitive 5%

Sensory 9%

Medical 28%

Physical 58%

DISABILITY AND POVERTY

Approximately a third of all disabled Americans live at or near the poverty level, according to the 2000 NOD/Harris Survey of Americans with Disabilities (May-June 2000). Forty-six percent of the households of single mothers receiving Temporary Assistance to Needy Families (TANF) aid have a disability or a disabled child; 38 percent of these single mothers are disabled, as the chart below shows.[1] The majority of those receiving the minimum food stamp benefit of $10 per month are people with disabilities whose health is in jeopardy due to lack of adequate nutrition.[2] Less than 26 percent of state and local housing agencies see housing for people with disabilities as a priority.[3]

Notes

1 Sunhwa Lee, Melissa Sills, and Gi-Taik Oh, "Disabilities Among Children and Mothers in Low-Income Families," *Research-in-Brief*, Publication #D449 (Washington, DC: Institute for Women's Policy Research, 2002).

2 Northwest Federation of Community Organizations, *Food Stamps Out Hunger* (August 2001).

3 Ann O'Hara and Emily Miller, *Going It Alone: The Struggle to Expand Housing Opportunities for People with Disabilities*, (Technical Assistance Collaboration and the Consortium for Citizens with Disabilities Housing Task Force, 2001).

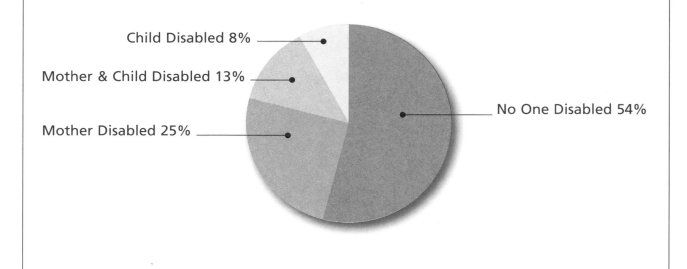

Child Disabled 8%

Mother & Child Disabled 13%

Mother Disabled 25%

No One Disabled 54%

DISABILITY AND ABUSE

People with disabilities become victims of violence at a rate greatly disproportionate to those without disabilities:

- A national survey indicates that 62 percent of women with disabilities will be emotionally, physically, or sexually assaulted at some point in their lives.[1]

- Adults with disabilities are four to ten times more likely to be victims of sexual abuse than the general population. Children with disabilities are 200 percent more likely to be physically or sexually abused than non-disabled children.[2]

- One study notes that in 96 percent of abuse cases of abuse of people with disabilities, the perpetrator was known to the victim; 44 percent of the perpetrators were service providers, and 79 percent of the individuals were victimized more than once.[3]

- Disabilities often prevent escape from and reporting of such attacks. One study reports that in 73 percent of the cases, adequate services were not offered.[4]

Notes

1 Joint survey conducted by Violence Against Women Office (VAWO) of Office of Justice Programs, U.S. Department of Justice, and Minnesota Center Against Violence and Abuse (MINCAVA) of the University of Minnesota. For further information, e-mail *info@vaw.umn.edu*.

2 Dick Sobsey, *Violence and Abuse in the Lives of People with Disabilities: The End of Silent Acceptance*? (Baltimore, MD: Paul H. Brookes Publishing, 1994), 269.

3 Dick Sobsey and T. Doe, "Patterns of Sexual Abuse and Assault," *Sexuality and Disability* (1991) 9:3: 243-260.

4 Sobsey and Doe, "Patterns of Sexual Abuse and Assault."

DISABILITY AND EMPLOYMENT[1]

- Only 19 percent of people with significant disabilities are working full-time, although 72 percent would like a job.

- Fifty-five percent of disabled college graduates are unemployed, compared to 14 percent of non-disabled graduates.

- Eight-five and a half percent of significantly disabled African Americans and 75.4 percent of significantly disabled Hispanics are unemployed.

- Employment opportunities are limited by such factors as lack of dependable accessible transportation.

- Sixty-four percent of adults with disabilities reported encountering active discrimination in seeking employment. Of those working,

  — 40 percent were denied workplace accommodations, 75 percent of which would cost under $500

  — 29 percent were paid less than others in similar jobs

  — 32 percent were given less responsibility than co-workers

---

Note

1 2000 NOD/Harris Survey of Americans with Disabilities; Louis Harris and Associates, *ICD Survey of Disabled Americans: Bringing Disabled Americans into the Mainstream* (New York, 1986).

Appendix A
Resources for Opening Doors of Welcome and Justice

BISHOPS' STATEMENTS AND OTHER USCCB RESOURCES

Pastoral Statement of U.S. Catholic Bishops on Persons with Disabilities. By the United States Conference of Catholic Bishops (USCCB) (Washington, DC: USCCB, 1978; revised edition, 2002). Available from USCCB Publishing (800-235-8722); ask for Pub. No. 5-424.

In this 1978 document, the bishops called for "a deeper understanding of both the pain and the potential of our neighbors who are blind, deaf, mentally disabled, emotionally impaired; who have special learning problems; or who suffer from single or multiple physical disabilities" (no. 1). They asserted, "On the most basic level, the Church responds to persons with disabilities by defending their rights" (no. 7).

Welcome and Justice for Persons with Disabilities: A Framework of Access and Inclusion. By the USCCB (Washington, DC: USCCB, 1995). Available from USCCB Publishing (800-235-8722); ask for Pub. No. 5-311.

This concise summary of the major themes of the 1978 pastoral statement commemorates its twentieth anniversary and fosters access and inclusion of people with various disabilities in the life of the Church and society.

Guidelines for the Celebration of the Sacraments with Persons with Disabilities. By the USCCB (Washington, DC: USCCB, 1995). Available from USCCB Publishing (800-235-8722); ask for Pub. No. 5-425.

The issue of access to all the sacraments is explored in this challenging call to create meaningful inclusion: "The creation of a fully accessible parish reaches beyond mere physical accommodation to encompass the attitudes of all parishioners toward persons with disabilities. Pastoral ministers are encouraged to develop

53

specific programs aimed at forming a community of believers known for its joyful inclusion of all of God's people around the table of the Lord" (no. 6).

In the Footsteps of Jesus: Catholic Social Teaching at Work Today (28-minute video). By the USCCB Department of Social Development and World Peace (Washington, DC: USCCB, 2003). Available from USCCB Publishing (800-235-8722); ask for Pub. No. 5-444 (English); No. 5-891 (Spanish).

> How is God calling you to follow in the footsteps of Jesus and put his teachings into practice in the world? Teenagers, young adults, small faith communities, and those interested in social justice will be challenged to respond to this core question. The video includes a study guide.

Leader's Guide to "Sharing Catholic Social Teaching." By the USCCB Committees on International Policy, on Domestic Policy, and on Education (Washington, DC: USCCB, 2000). Available from USCCB Publishing (800-235-8722); ask for Pub. No. 5-366.

> Ideal for religious educators at the diocesan and parish levels, this guide was developed to assist parish ministers and other adults in studying Catholic social teaching.

Special Needs Resource Directory: Let the Children Come to Me. By the USCCB Department of Education (Washington, DC: USCCB, ongoing). Available on the USCCB website: *www. usccb.org/education/fedasst/idea.htm*; click on "Special Needs Directory."

> This resource responds to the call to embrace and serve children with special needs in Catholic schools and parish religious education programs.

Information on the Individuals with Disabilities Education Act (IDEA). By the USCCB Department of Education (Washington, DC: USCCB, ongoing). Available on the USCCB website: *www.usccb.org/education/fedasst/idea.htm*.

> This webpage provides information on the IDEA, a law that, when originally drafted in 1975, authorized the federal government to provide up to 40 percent of the total cost for special education; this webpage also provides ongoing information on reauthorizations of the IDEA.

VATICAN STATEMENTS AND RESOURCES

Vatican statements and resources on persons with disabilities, from the 2000 Jubilee Day of the Community of Persons with Disabilities, can be found at the Vatican website: *www.vatican.va/ jubilee_2000/jubilevents/events_ jubildisabled_en.htm*.

NATIONAL CATHOLIC PARTNERSHIP ON DISABILITY

NCPD Poverty Brochure. By the National Catholic Partnership on Disability (NCPD) (Washington, DC: NCPD, 2003). Available from the NCPD (202-529-2933); $0.45 each; $35.00 for bundle of 100).

This four-color, ten-panel brochure offers brief but significant information on demographics, poverty, abuse, unemployment, health care, and other issues.

Opening Doors to People with Disabilities. By the NCPD (Washington, DC: NCPD, 1996). Available from the NCPD (202-529-2933); priced as indicated below.

Volume 1: Pastoral Manual. This 215-page manual provides specific information in a concise, easy-to-read format. Chapters and topics in this volume are coordinated with the those in Volume II, The Resource File. Also available on audio cassette. For 1-9 copies, $12.00 each; 10 or more copies, $10.50 each.

Volume 2: The Resource File. This 1,400-page encyclopedia is neatly packaged in two loose-leaf binders (Book A and Book B) to provide flexibility in research and in planning for workshops and conferences. Also available on audio cassette. For 1-9 copies, $50.00 each; for 10 or more copies, $45.00 each.

Two-Volume Set. Also available on audio cassette. For 1-9 sets, $55.00 each; for 10 or more sets, $50.00 each.

A Loving Justice: The Moral and Legal Responsibilities of the U.S. Catholic Church Under the Americans with Disabilities Act. By the NCPD (Washington, DC: NCPD, 1995). Available from the NCPD (202-529-2933); 1-9 copies, $7.50 each; 10 or more copies, $6.50 each.

This 58-page, user-friendly, practical guide covers the requirements of church entities by the landmark civil rights legislation for people with disabilities: the 1990 Americans with Disabilities Act. Also available in large-print format and on audio cassette.

Disability Ministry: Perspectives on Disability (29-minute video; open captioned). By the NCPD (Washington, DC: NCPD, 1996). Available from the NCPD (202-529-2933); $10.00 each.

This video is useful in stimulating group discussion and awareness and features NCPD Executive Director Mary Jane Owen in a series of vignettes, which may be used separately if desired. Topics include definition of disability, demographics of disability, perspective on the paralyzed man from Capernaum (Mk 2:1-12), theological implications of disability, the value of every life, and Blessed Margaret of Castello.

OTHER CATHOLIC DISABILITY MATERIALS

National Catholic Office for the Deaf
Visit *www.ncod.org* and click on "NCOD Catalogue" for a complete listing of resources and ordering information.

Network of Inclusive Catholic Educators: University of Dayton Institute for Pastoral Initiatives
Visit *www.udayton.edu/ ~ipi/nice/index.php3* and click on "Resources" for a complete listing of videos and prints resources and ordering information.

CURRICULA

Rose Fitzgerald Kennedy Program to Improve Catholic Religious Education for Children and Adults with Mental Retardation
Developed by the Diocese of Pittsburgh, this comprehensive Catholic religious education program is written in a developmental mode and is appropriate for use in the inclusive classroom, the specialized classroom, or the home. Contains a manual for catechists, 260 lesson plans and prayer services, a handbook for parents, resources, and references to Scripture, the *Catechism of the Catholic Church,* and *Sharing the Light of Faith: The National Catechetical Directory.* This program and other special-education resources are available from Silver Burdett Ginn Religion, 800-522-2259; *www.sbgreligion.com*.

Catechesis of the Good Shepherd
The Association of the Catechesis of the Good Shepherd offers an approach to the religious formation of children; the approach, which is "rooted in the Bible, the liturgy of the Church, and the educational principles of Maria Montessori," may be adapted for use with children with disabilities. Contact the Association of the Catechesis of the Good Shepherd, P.O. Box 1084, Oak Park, IL 60304; 708-524-1210; *www.cgsusa.org*.

Journey with Jesus
For this sacramental preparation curriculum resource for people with cognitive disabilities, contact Cardinal Stritch University Bookstore, 6801 North Yates Road, Box 501, Milwaukee, WI 53217; 414-410-4035; *www.stritch.edu*.

SPRED (Special Religious Development)
SPRED includes specialized training focused on helping persons with cognitive disabilities to participate in worship through the process of education in their faith. Contact Archdiocese of Chicago, SPRED Center, 2956 South Lowe Avenue, Chicago, IL 60616; 312-842-1039; *www.spred.org*.

NATIONAL CATHOLIC ORGANIZATIONS

CUSA: An Apostolate of the Chronically Sick and Disabled

CUSA offers friendship, encouragement and support to disabled and chronically ill people. Services include exchange of group letters, magazine, cassette tapes and books and articles, and annual days of recollection. Contact Anna Marie Sopko, 176 W. 8th Street, Bayonne, NJ 07002-1227; *www.cusan.org*.

Faith and Fellowship

This program offers spiritual, catechetical, and social outreach for adults who experience mental illness. For many, it provides entrée into the life and activities of the parish; for others, it is an opportunity for spiritual growth tailored to their unique and often fragile situation. Training and materials are provided to parishes or dioceses wishing to provide this ministry. Contact Connie Rakitan, 38 North Austin Blvd., Oak Park, IL 60302; 708-383-9276; *cmr1551@comcast.net*.

Faith and Light

This international movement offers support to people with developmental disabilities, their families, and friends. Community gatherings provide opportunities for faith sharing, celebrating, and prayer. Visit their website at *www.faithandlight.net*.

Faith and Sharing

This Jean Vanier–style summer retreat fosters the experience of Christian community and church, involving young and old—married, single, and religious. Persons with disabilities are at the heart of the experience. For further information, visit *www.faithandsharing.faithweb.com*.

Mark Seven Deaf Foundation

The foundation offers a variety of camp programs in upper-state New York for children and adults who are deaf, as well as religious vocation programs and an intensive camp for training in American Sign Language. Visit *www.campmark7.org*.

National Apostolate for Inclusion Ministry (NAfIM)

Calling together persons with and without mental retardation, NAfIM witnesses to the Good News that all persons are created in God's image and likeness. The apostolate promotes the full incorporation of persons with mental retardation and their gifts into the Body of Christ, as proclaimed by the teachings of the Catholic Church. Contact NAfIM, P.O. Box 218, Riverdale, MD 20738; 301-699-9500 or toll-free 800-736-1280; *www.nafim.org*.

National Catholic Bioethics Center (NCBC)

The mission of the National Catholic Bioethics Center is to promote and safeguard the dignity of the human person through research, education, consultation, and publishing in the health and life sciences for private individuals, bishops, priests, physicians, nurses, hospital administrators, and those who shape law and public policy. Contact NCBC, 159 Washington Street, Boston, MA 02135; 617-787-1900; *www.ncbcenter.org*.

National Catholic Educational Association (NCEA)

NCEA provides seminars and consultations on special educational services. Contact NCEA, Early Childhood and Special Educational Services, 1077 30th Street, NW, Suite 100, Washington, DC 20007-3852; 202-337-6232; *www.ncea.org*.

National Catholic Office for the Deaf (NCOD)

NCOD is a non-profit membership organization dedicated to pastoral ministry with deaf and hard-of-hearing persons. This pastoral ministry offers deaf Catholics services and support that fosters spiritual development in their own language. Contact NCOD, 7202 Buchanan St., Landover Hills, MD 20784; 301-577-1684, TTY 301-577-4184; *www.ncod.org*.

National Catholic Partnership on Disability (NCPD)

Formerly the National Catholic Office for Persons with Disabilities, NCPD was established to further implementation of the 1978 Pastoral Statement of U.S. Catholic Bishops on People with Disabilities. Among its various information resources is Opening Doors to People with Disabilities: a two-volume resource with more than 1,600 pages dedicated to promoting inclusion of persons with disabilities in the life of the Church. Contact NCPD, McCormick Pavilion, Suite 240, 415 Michigan Avenue, NE, Washington, DC 20017-4501; 202-529-2933, TTY 202-529-2934; *www.ncpd.org*.

National Federation for Catholic Youth Ministry (NFCYM)

NFCYM's disability task group created an online resource for youth with disabilities, which can be found on its website at *www.nfcym.org*.

Network of Inclusive Catholic Educators: University of Dayton Institute of Pastoral Initiatives (NICE)

NICE serves as a support network and resource to individuals with disabilities and their families by providing conferences, video and print resources, consultations, workshops, and networking opportunities on the national and local level. Contact Institute for Pastoral Initiatives, University of Dayton, Dayton, OH 45469; 937-229-4356 or toll-free 888-532-3389; *www.udayton.edu/~ipi/nice/index.php3*.

Victorious Missionaries

This spiritual movement by and for disabled and chronically ill people offers monthly days of renewal, retreats, and a bimonthly newsletter. Contact Victorious Missionaries, National Shrine of Our Lady of the Snows, 442 South Demazenod, Belleville, IL 62223; 618-397-6700 (voice/TTY); *www.vmusa.org*.

Xavier Society for the Blind

Free materials are mailed directly to visually impaired and deaf-blind persons in Braille, large-print format, or audio cassette; lending library service is offered in all three media. Contact Xavier Society for the Blind, 154 East 23rd St., New York, NY 10010; 212-473-7800 or toll-free 800-637-9193.

FEDERAL GOVERNMENT AGENCIES

National Council on Disability: *www.ncd.gov*

U.S. Department of Education Office for Civil Rights: *www.ed.gov/offices/OCR*

U.S. Department of Education Office of Special Education: *www.ed.gov/offices/OSERS/OSEP*

U.S. Department of Housing and *Urban Development: www.hud.gov*

U.S. Department of Justice, Civil Rights *Division: www.usdoj.gov/crt*

U.S. Department of Labor, Office of Disability Employment Policy: *www.dol.gov/odep*

U.S. Equal Employment Opportunity *Commission: www.eeoc.gov*

COPIES OF PUBLIC LAWS

The Americans with Disabilities Act of 1990 (P.L. 101-336), the Individuals with Disabilities Education Act (IDEA) (P.L. 101-476), the reauthorization of IDEA (P.L. 105-117), and similar disability laws are available at *thomas.loc.gov*.

Appendix B
Questions to Be Included in a Parish Census or Registration Form

People, including aging individuals, often may not identify themselves as having a disability even though they have diminished mobility, vision, and hearing that can be greatly enhanced by railings or ramps, adequate lighting, or hearing enhancement systems. The questions below, when asked of everyone in the parish, can provide helpful information in planning for appropriate access. Care should be taken to locate and survey people who may not be currently active in the parish.

1. Are you able to attend Mass?
   ❑ Y   ❑ N

   If not, please specify reason:

2. Please check any of the following that would enhance your ability to participate fully in the life of the parish:

   ❑ Transportation
   ❑ Large-print hymnals and/or missalettes
   ❑ Sign-language interpreter
   ❑ Braille hymnals and/or missalettes
   ❑ Oral interpreter
   ❑ Increased lighting
   ❑ Cassette tape
   ❑ Real-time captioning
   ❑ Hearing device
   ❑ Welcoming companion
   ❑ Accessible:
      ❑ entrance
      ❑ sanctuary
      ❑ restroom
      ❑ parking space

Please mention any other needs.

4. Do you wish to receive preparation for any of the following sacrament(s)?
   ❑ Baptism
   ❑ Matrimony
   ❑ Eucharist
   ❑ Confirmation
   ❑ Reconciliation

5. How do you wish to contribute to the life of the parish community (e.g., lector, choir member, catechist, parish council, etc.)?